AMERIKAN Honey

Requiem for a Nightmare

by

Alexander Tesfaye

The contents of this work, including, but not limited to, the accuracy of events, people, and places depicted; opinions expressed; permission to use previously published materials included; and any advice given or actions advocated are solely the responsibility of the author, who assumes all liability for said work and indemnifies the publisher against any claims stemming from publication of the work.

All Rights Reserved
Copyright © 2024 by Alexander Tesfaye

No part of this book may be reproduced or transmitted, downloaded, distributed, reverse engineered, or stored in or introduced into any information storage and retrieval system, in any form or by any means, including photocopying and recording, whether electronic or mechanical, now known or hereinafter invented without permission in writing from the publisher.

Dorrance Publishing Co
585 Alpha Drive
Suite 103
Pittsburgh, PA 15238
Visit our website at *www.dorrancebookstore.com*

ISBN: 979-8-88812-143-6
eISBN: 979-8-88812-643-1

Dedicated and Special Thanks to

My Teacher Friend
an **Extraterrestrial**
and a **Sunflower**

Jibber Jabber

Jermaine Cole

My body feels suspended as if my spine was tethered to the clouds
I look out in hope of an escape and see Dante's ninth circle of hell
Looking out into what will soon be my death,
I think over things that I regret
I always felt immortal, yet I will fall victim to what has been the death of many of my brothers and sisters
The impact sends shrapnel into the air (my tethers snapped)

In this throne that was promised to be fit for a king,
I gaze upon the beauty of the sky
The freedoms that the sky promises are almost addicting
The ability to dance across the sky
in choreographed movements with the clouds
To unlock the secrets hidden in the stars whilst you go on adventures with the man on the moon
To have people see you as something truly beautiful.

I'm a Ghost; Who are You?

I'm a ghost; who are you?

Are you...a...ghost as well?

hiding in the Lonely Soul's closet through the night!

Scaring the living with fright!

Oh, the pain of being...alive.

The stress of not being thought of or missed!

All these terrible thoughts running through your head!

Oh, how happy I am that we are...dead.

I am alone

I am alone the way a deaf kid tumbles into a school classroom

I am alone in the way a blind kid can't read braille, the way they feel the patterns but can't pick up the words

I am alone

My friends fill the empty edges of a mirror

My friends are the sunken wrinkles in an old man's skin

My friends mix together the same way orange juice concentrate meets with gasoline

My friends are the razor blades used by the local barber to get the closest shave

We are lost.

Bloody Sheets

The deep crimson splashes across the soft linen forming branches

She cries out only to have silence respond back

Her eyes meet that of materialism

The glare makes her stomach drop

The blade sinks into her throat

She drowns in her Versace bags and exclusive dinner reservations

Enlightenment

Empathetic senses got me stressin' like a groom second-guessing his vows

A soul-crushing religious creed built on the foundation of excellence formed by Freemasons and Egyptian pharaohs

My skin feels like a suit tailored for the wrong body

My tongue feels misplaced

My eyes don't fit their sockets

Carving hieroglyphs in my skin in hopes of communicating with a higher power

For the goals I've set for my children will only be reached with sacrificial blood

Saints and heretics alike will join arms for the revival

For our Age of Enlightenment remains in between the text we have censored from our children

We will heed the warnings our founding fathers made known

For the laws of Malcolm X and the sins of our fathers are now consuming the hearts of our children

Soon the lepers and sex offenders will look to us with watery eyes seeking redemption

Begging and pleading

And we will answer

No

A Beautiful Moment

Hands stuck to the steering wheel like a parasite to its host.

Her hands ran through my hair like a flock of birds migrating

The light from the moon cast upon the hood of the car like God's hand reaching down from heaven.

Words pass along each other's tongues like a colony of ants lost in the grass.

A song is picked out for nostalgic purposes.

Vocal cords stretch to let out off-key notes.

In a beautiful moment, we found ourselves comfortable enough to take each other's hand and dance as if no one was watching

Slowed movements reminiscent of Matt Damon in *Eurotrip*.

In a moment of laughter, I realized this was a moment I would never forget.

Key

Two-toned, two-face serpent located on the innermost portions of my body

Works as a lockpick for the door you've protected for so long.

Deal with the Devil

A deal was made

A soul was sold

Leaving the body with the steam collecting on the windows

Sins committed

Screams escape

Bloodshed on leather seats

The radio turned on max so no one passing by would have an idea

Tears fall while he has his hand around her throat

Trying to gasp for air, she calls out his name

Control

Ever since I was a child I found that lack of power in a room was more bone-crushing than a fistfight
That scarcity of management would take your breath faster than any bullet
That absence of authority will devour you like the monsters that swell your father's belly

It was small things,
The TV
The video game
What meal we ate

As I grow older it follows
It spreads like a virus through a decaying body
It spreads like corruption in a church
It eats away at what's left of my brain

Now it's something much more
No no
This demon would make an atheist pray for Jesus
This behemoth would make a kingdom cry wolf
This,
Lack
Of …

Control

It's everywhere

No matter where I look
It's in my hair
On my skin
In my pocket
In my relationship
At my job
Seeping through my veins like tears watering the garden that is the graveyard of my dreams
I need

Control.

False Reality

I feel isolated in a simulated state
like a boy in a bubble under the ocean
chasing oxygen that was never there to begin with
like a detective trying to solve a case when he himself was the murderer

When our sins are weighed against our souls do you think we still earn a place amongst the angels?
Do we still have a place in the heavens?

Because how could a sinful creature as I deserve a spot in the same place of residency as someone like Robin Williams?

I often ponder if the celebrities we idolize were ever real to begin with

This fabricated reality airbrushed onto postcards and billboards
We worship hollow shells and empty eyes

I feel a disconnect with the world
like an animal with short-term memory loss

what does a bird do when it forgets the basic instinct of migration?

Even Lucifer was Angelic

Power, Sex, and Sin

Gunshots ring in my head

Tremors crawl through my body like lightning in the sky

The sins I've committed are unforgivable

I await my Judgment Day.

My god stands before me, her eyes filled with rage

She asks why I have done what I did

I look back at her and say, "For what is a god to a nonbeliever?"

She pulls the trigger and blood seeps into the ground beneath me

Queen of Hearts

I stand in the pale moonlight slow dancing to the latest tune stuck in my head
My moves were choreographed for the children of the forest to spectate
As I begin my third set, the spotlight turns to the center of the forest
The creatures turn their attention to the Queen of Hearts wrapped in the glistening glow of the light
Her beautiful stature draws us all closer
The kids begin to salivate as she begins her samba
Rage builds inside me but heading for the throne is a far cry
Dressed in motley, looking like the king's jester
I step upon her red carpet
She laughs and makes a gesture toward her guards
I am beheaded
The children clap and cheer

Suicide, a poem

The difference between this poem and our suicide note is...
I wrote this hoping it would never find you.

You stand in front of me with the stature of a glass sculpture—
Beautiful and made with the precision of a laser, focused but lethal.
Yet so fragile that something as simple as the phrase, "I need you,"
will make you shatter.

When I met you in that dream of mine, I found myself cast into the ocean, helpless.
Drowning in this sea of my own tears.
Tears used to clean the sins of my past.
Tears used to wash away the misconceptions of love.

Feet tied to the sinking ship that is our relationship—
You had no idea exactly what you were doing to me.

Josh Katz said, "She's in my head again," but I find myself begging for you to come back.

See, in between subtle conversation and crushing text messages,
I lost grip of what was "us."

You took my wings and soared through the sky like a missile that lost its track.
You're dangerous the same way an objection is at a wedding.
You're scary the way "I love you" is too early in a relationship.

But somehow beautiful...the way your breakfast tastes after a near-death experience.

To put it simply, you're my newfound addiction that no 12-step program can help!
But then I sit and ask myself, am I ready to let you go?

Psycho

When looking into this shattered mirror, I can see what once was myself
I am now nothing, but an idea, a memory.
See, Alexander Tesfaye used to be something real, alive, earthly.

And although you can feel my flesh or hear my voice when I speak, I have become the ghost at the back of your closet.

I am now the fine line between "American Dream" and "American Psycho."
See, she claims I'm a sociopath, but that's just not true
How can I be a sociopath when I have so much love for myself?

I count the footsteps of those in front of me, 1, 2, 3... 1, 2, 3
This sequence resembling Poe's unbearable ticking
1, 2, 3... 1, 2, 3
Blood flows beneath their shoes and I salivate at the view.

My family claims I'm a narcissist, but how can that be when I feel no emotion at all?
I see death in the street and have no remorse.
I pull the trigger and don't even flinch.

My therapist says I'm schizophrenic, but how is that possible if I have no friends?
Sometimes the weight of my loneliness crushes my lungs.
It's so bad the doctors have to put me on a ventilator just so I can breathe.

The oxygen leaves my body and personifies itself as the next serial killer of a Netflix documentary.
The blade it carries doesn't cut flesh.
No, this weapon wields something much more destructive.
No, this blade carves secrets into my reputation.
The sharp edge engraving the thoughts I have into my arm
showing the world exactly what I am.
This blade reveals the skeleton that lies beneath the surface of my persona.

So I ask again, how can I be a narcissist if I feel no emotion?
How can I be a sociopath if I have so much love for myself?
How can I be schizophrenic if my doctors tell me I'm alone?

Ghost Town

Fingertips strike like lightning
The fire erupts on my skin
These flames light the room and scare away the darkness
I can't feel my face

You tell me not to fall but loosen my grip
You tell me I'm safe but load your gun
You tell me it'll be okay, but tears are running down your face
You tell me that we are healthy, but I am dying

You stopped me on my way out
I was scared that you were leaving
You made me happy for a moment; then you would be gone
Why did you kiss me?

You know they say that we got our gold and silver from two stars colliding into each other
I got to thinking about it and we have a similar chemistry
Except when we collided, it didn't end with precious metals treasured by all
No, we ended with scars and broken records

This empty room sounds of a ghost town
The same song playing on repeat
The same words were spoken with the same rhythm
Yet I sit in this corner alone expecting a different outcome

Whispers in the Dark

You whisper in my ear leading me down a rabbit hole
I find myself consumed by my own thoughts
The words you speak wrap me in a blanket of anxiety and fear
You tell me it's okay and let me go

The corners of the room provide a safe space to hide, for the light cannot reach you there
Your hand cradles mine like a magazine holding a 9mm.
Our souls chase one another
Like a game of cat and mouse

The touch of your fingertips on my chest entices me to let you in
Your lips meet mine to cause a chain reaction leading to rapture
I hear the rattle of bones from your closet
if ignorance is bliss, may I never find peace

Purgatory

The darkness that surrounds me can only be cured by the purity of another
The fear of being alone has consumed me
A beast conjured by ancient heretics, even God could not save me

Communicating with darker forces, I find myself trapped in a cycle, my own purgatory

She lays beside me, comfortable, happy
I wrap my sinful arms around her composed stature as fleeting gesture of gentleness
she caresses my chest as we both lay there exposed to the demons that follow us

So close I can feel her heartbeat against my chest
She kisses my forehead as I lay on her chest. I miss these moments with you that only took place in the confines of my mind

I awake, in a bed, alone

Naturally I message you in hopes of finding some comfort in this bleak situation, yet I am left with nothing more than dry text

You haven't the slightest idea of what you caused.

I love when we pass each other in the hall

It's like I'm

F

A

L

L

I

N

G

all over again

I've Been Going Through Something

Trapped in this cell reminiscent of White Ferrari with Nostalgia airbrushed on the fender
A Bender on my own Conspiracies has led me to the point of not even recognizing my past
So lost in between these dreams and visions
Reality is growing hazy

The silhouette of the demon from my past sits before me
Her wine glass full of the blood-soaked memories we share
Her nails tap the marble table
A rhythm mimicking a death march

She speaks of our history commenting on the good times
These times filled with bruises on skin
Scratches on flesh
Used bodies

Times filled with questions like,
"Wyd?" at 2:00 a.m.
or "what position" while her parents were asleep in the other room
maybe even, "Is this all you wanted?"

She laughs as she swirls her cocktail filled with parties and blackouts, shotguns and tears

I catch my breath
I excuse myself and go to the bathroom
In a panic I wash my face

Looking up into the mirror, I do not recognize my reflection

No these eyes do not belong to me
This smirk does not fit my face
These horns
This forked tail...

The only way to overcome and defeat demons
is to become a devil yourself.

Ash

We find ourselves on a conveyor belt asking, "Mother, should we trust the government?"

These pills that we wash down with pesticides bloom as weeds in our stomach.

They fill with the fruit of our ancestors.

We feast upon the corpses of our fallen brothers, chanting old songs as if to celebrate.

If you overheard my conversations with the man in the mirror, you would put me down like a dog in the street.

Oh, to have a gun to your head.

To feel the adrenaline of knowing your life lies in the hands of someone whose sole intent is to end it.

How freeing that must be!

One may find it cynical, but with ash being our truest form, how could you question your outcome?

To rejoin the earth as it consumes you—to feed your children.

Why would you want anything more?

Snake Oil

Our Savior

Awkward stances in narrow hallways
Sunken faces with exhausted expressions
Each murmuring Old English cursing their gods for the situation they're in
Rage flowing through their body the way insults pass around a schoolyard.

Behind me, I hear a rather loud bewildering man
Complaining about something to do with taxes and God's divine plan.
He asks to bum a cigarette off me, I ignore him
A woman steps up and gives him what he demands.

Blackened teeth marking the sunken face with dark bags under his eyes
Baggy, worn-down clothes fitting his scrawny stature
Glasses hanging down his nose giving the impression that he cares about his appearance as much as he cares for his liver.

Speaking in tongues, he tells me that he is the one and only savior and that I will be damned to hell for not helping him.
He, himself, will lead the people to the new world and guide us from darkness.
In a profound speech, he says he is above us all, saying he was appointed to save us.

I interrupt to ask him for proof.
At this moment a tear falls from his eye

His pores begin to swell as liquor and pills burst from his skin.
Dark potent concoctions spill on the floor beneath us
His flesh begins to melt into the ground as he speaks in tongues.

The floor beneath me opens and the earth swallows me whole.

Somehow even in death, he takes from me what he couldn't provide me in the first place....

Your cocaine promises and drunken texts
fuel my reasons to improve.

Seppuku

When contemplating suicide one tends to think about what rope would make a suitable noose for them.

What razor blade defines them as a person?

Which firearm will paint their mural perfectly?

At least this is what I'm told.
Many different accounts taken from mirrors on bathroom walls
Finding yourself stuck in a limbo, drowning in your sins
Dripping ichor, you feel enlightened.

Looking through the eye of Horus, you begin to understand the sacred geometry
The rules of 3.6.9.
You unlock the secrets of the universe from ingredients on the back of a chewing gum wrapper.

Welcome to salivation

Only once one loses everything are they free to do anything

American Honey

In the confines of a suicide cell, you made a decision that would impact the world with a ripple.
"Son, it is always about a girl."
Then why am I writing this about you?
The sunken wrinkles of your face that fall deep as the Mariana Trench tell a story.
Coming from the foundation of rape and molestation, you emerged a powerful warrior with a sword made of Percocet and smoke.
Your shield? Wild Turkey and Mad Dog 2020.
I often wonder what your life would have been like if someone truly loved you, but those pills held you close and helped you bloom.
Like an acrobat on a tightrope made of angel hair
walking over a pit of elongated needles you ran.
Your legs like wooden wheels on a wagon, arms like twigs, and body like powdered milk.
You kept running, running away from the demons, the monsters, the people, the guilt, the memories, you just kept running, running until you fell.
As a devil dog, your pride seeped deep into your skin like tar.
Asking for help was not an option.
Changing yourself was not even a part of the equation.
Because what is it they say? Once you hit rock bottom the only way is up, right?
You challenged that saying heading toward the bottom with the speed of a shooting star.
Hiding away in church like a bunny in the bushes, you awaited your fate.

You knew it was coming.
The wolf towered in the sky like an obelisk.
You were afraid, but pride would not allow you to stop it.
Four years have passed
You still remain in that trailer
Those wrinkles still lie deep in your skin.

Sincerely Yours,
your beautiful boy

Martyr

I'm brushing my teeth with a straight razor
The blood seeps from the blade
The droplets splash, tainting Genesis
The ichor burns on the aged pages
The protruding light from the transparent glass above begins to take form in the shape of a serpent
The beast constricts around my neck
I attempt to use my blade, but it crumbles like aluminum
The room begins to darken as the oxygen escapes from my lungs
I am nothing but a martyr.

Shame

Sleep deprivation has me philosophical
Seeing new dimensions through my heavy eyelids
Worlds colliding right before me in third period
Galaxies collapsing in fifth
In these nights filled with insomnia and dread of the unknown, I find peace in the fantasies I construct
A portal allowing me to escape from the world I remain
Her hands wrap around my skull like a safety net to catch me when I fall
The liquid love I consumed to keep my body warm on the cold nights alone has left me desperate
The test before me reads positive, eyes tearing up, trust lost
My mother ashamed
I seek answers....

Poetic Philosophy

When facing a loaded gun, you begin to ponder all sorts of things like...
What kind of bullet casing defines me as a person?
Will the spatter stain my carpet?
Will the red at least match the shoes I'm wearing?

Nihilism consumes your brain and ravages your thoughts.
Disassociation fills the mind with potent ideas and dreams.
Escaping reality.

I can still taste the sulfur.
Smoke escapes my mouth like jumbled words being regurgitated in front of your crush.
The ringing is a repertoire of crying children.
The flash from the muzzle lights every corner of the room like an atom bomb.
Entire universe reduced to ash by the death of one.

Some Facts about Me

I was born on Dec 7th, 2004, which means that I really don't like surprises...sorry that was cheesy
I like horror movies
My favorite drink is an Arnold Palmer
I will argue that *Watchmen* is the greatest comic book movie of all time
And will debate that Mac Miller's "Swimming" and TheWeeknds' "After Hours" were co-produced by angels

Y'know there seems to be a few common traits in my family: substance abuse, tattoos, and divorce to name a few
Which is to say that we have an easier time committing to needles and bottles filled with any substance than we do to relationships...

Jake Gyllenhaal is my favorite actor
And Rudy Francisco and r.h. Sin remain my inspiration
Texas Chainsaw Massacre will always be a classic, but *Scream* is the better slasher

I am the son of a devil dog covered in snake oil who builds his philosophies on lyrics from Bob Dylan and The Talking Heads

I am the son of a sunflower who can capture the Milky Way in the confines of her heart, truly a pure soul.

For as long as I can remember, I've had a thing for girls with cute smiles and tattoos
My favorite item of clothing is a crewneck

Marilyn Manson was my idol growing up
And Stephen King's writing has taught me to stop looking for the monsters under my bed but instead look for them in the values of men

I have always liked superheroes
Now it may seem nerdy but everyone can relate to heroes
Everyone wants some power to either solve problems or just for the freedom
And whata freedom like the freedom of flight
Because heroes fly!

And as a child I was always warned of the horrors you may experience with that freedom
My father always stood as a symbol of heroism, leading me on great adventures
Slaying dragons and discovering foreign planets
But as I continue to grow, I learned that my hero still chases that freedom of flight

I miss you.

Mary Shelley

In my room, you will find suicide notes lodged in old bottles of alcohol
A religious creed that no matter the pain of his absence, maybe if I can find something we have in common, he would strike up a conversation.

Maybe...
just maybe a reason for him to stay.

The best storytellers are Recovering Drug Addicts.

Lights, Camera, Action!

Acting is to play a fictional role in a play, film, or television series

What a career
Being able to play the role of so many different lives
Genuinely limitless potential
You want to be a Roman Emperor? How bout that childhood dream of being an astronaut? Maybe even a legendary space wizard with a plasma sword? You could do it all

A career that gives you the option to escape the life you hate to build any life you want

For me personally, I'd like to change myself just a little
Work on a new accent
Maybe be a bit more buff
Possibly change my political views
and with enough practice and just a little research
Maybe, just maybe I could play the role of the child that was worth staying for
Maybe the role of a child that my dad actually wanted

The Sins of Our Fathers

A generational curse passed down a hunger for possession and pleasure like it was hereditary

This hunger matches that of the insects that feed on my morality

This feeling—no that's not right; this instinct consumes my subconscious

This beast eats away at the remaining innocence left by the heroin dealers and politicians

It feels lethal.

Art

Visions of you from my past life attack the back of my mind the way a leopard stalks their prey.
Subtle moments of déjà vu.
A phantom smell of your perfume.
An aftertaste of your lips after a sip of wine.
A cold chill down my spine like your fingertips dancing on my skin.

Sometimes I feel the warmth of your tongue when their blood splatters on my face.
A twisted Jackson Pollock—now this, ladies and gentlemen, is art.
How can someone claim to have captured their likeness on canvas if they haven't seen the life leave their eyes?
Now that, children, is where I find God
because only in the presence of Death, can you feel something like God.

Where Did You Sleep Last Night?

Be Realistic

As you fall through a time warp
Looking through a kaleidoscope, reality tells a new story
The weight of your sins takes your breath
While you drown in the tears you've caused.

She stands in front of me piercing my soul with eyes like lost nebulas in this ocean of stars.
Her smile tethers me to the Earth, but as I try to fly, that same tether works as my anchor.
In daydreaming, the line between reality and imagination gets lost.
I swear to you, in the confines of my mind, we've already spent our life together, so why am I still nervous when you say, "Hi"?

I Wonder

When you bend over, do you arch your back the way you did for me?
When you moan, do you say their name the way you said mine?
Do your nails dig as deep?
I'm curious.
Do you talk to them the way you spoke to me
With clouds for words and rain for a voice?
Do you treat them the way you treated me?
Do you kiss their hand when they kiss your forehead?
Do you show them Montell Fish or r.h. Sin's poetry?
Do you hold them the way you held me?
I wonder what you think when my name is passed across the room?
Do you throw flirtatious actions like loose change?
Do you give your body like receipt paper?
Because no, you don't need that, but what you need is their affection.
I often ponder the power you would have if you thought you were just half as valuable as you are.
Your lack of self-worth hurts me more than any action you can do against me.
Did I not do a good enough job?
Was I not a good boyfriend?

File://103021

In between the restless nights of frigid despair
And long days of exhausting monologues to hollow shells
Twenty-four hours began to feel like a suggestion.

Like pen to paper, your lips tattoo the words I can't express onto my neck.
You sew hieroglyphics into my skin that tell an epic of lost treasure.
We found each other astray in our own fishbowl that Pink Floyd warned us of.

In a state of enlightenment, I find myself intertwined in the words you speak
Lost in every syllable leading me to wonderland.
I can't get enough of your voice, like the nectar of gods, it flows through my veins as lighting crawls in the sky.

Your laugh was intoxicating, speaking Hennessy words I could almost drown in between the pauses
Pupils dilated, I find myself swimming in your iris.
Holding your hand the way an artist takes their brush to canvas.
Nervous but precise,
Knowing that this very moment will stain our memories for a lifetime.

From morning sex to late-night talks,
From messy hair to bleeding back,
We find ourselves consumed in the conversation.

Oh it's back

That same haunted feeling of your lungs pushing the air out of your chest in hopes of finding peace in death.

The way that a knife feels when it meets perfect skin at its sharpest point.

The way teeth grind as the muzzle meets your temple.

That warm cozy feeling of blood flowing on your chest because your cries for help were quieter than your silence.

Your own thoughts consuming the abscess that surrounds them.

That animalistic need to paint a mural with brain matter.

I wonder how much that would be worth?

My life or theirs?

Rivener

My patience getting shorter like our text messages.
The carnal creature I built the foundation for has begun biting the hand that used to feed it.
A creature of primal instinct acting on the pure need for survival,
Cannibalistic nature mixed with suicidal thoughts and substance abuse,
Self-hate consumes you, dear.
You are my greatest failure.

Risk

I see the bountiful garden in you that is just waiting on the right care to blossom a fruitful harvest
I see in you the way a man lost in the desert views an oasis
What I see when I look at you is what a groom sees when the words "I do" rolls off their tongue
What I see in you is a risk worth taking,

Panic Attack in the AMC Theater Bathroom

The sins you committed run through my mind like a broken movie reel
For the lies of a friend will cost the life of a brother
How could you hide for so long?
Wolf in sheep's clothing, you carnal creature
A predator stalking prey
It only mattered when you were afraid of her leaving you
It only mattered when you saw me happy
It only mattered when you didn't get your way

Dear Love,

Honestly, I can't say for certain if I understand the meaning of the word.
Something about the concept never really sat right or made sense to me
It always seemed like something in the same category as Santa or the Easter Bunny, a fairy tale
Something your parents would tell you to make you look forward to your future
Something to distract you from bills and taxes
As I got older, I began to believe it was just chemicals pumping through your brain telling you that you and said person would create good offspring
Now that isn't to say that isn't the truth
I still find that to hold true
But,
Now
This
Is
A
Very
Big
But
When I look at you
In the morning
After a night of holding each other so close that we can feel each other's heartbeats
So close that we hang on to each other's exhales the way a diver holds on to oxygen

So close that we take every sound as a war drum calling the need for help
Love,
When I look at you
In the morning
After a night of rough sex and sweet talks
I find myself consumed by your iris
I don't know what love is, but I do hope that it is something like this.

For I am a Man

For I am a Man.
Sorrowful, I am not.

I stand broad.
A statue built upon the foundation of misogyny and religious persecution,
Drug addiction, and mental Illness.

For I am a Man.
My bones made strong from sexual coercion and domestic abuse.
Alcohol fuels the flames of my rage,
these flames so strong only the river from my spouse's eyes can dilute this hellfire.

For I am a Man.
These pitiful cries of pain sound to me like moans of pleasure.
These weak-minded children, how could you claim that?
You practically begged for it. Did you see what you were wearing?
We raise our boys with *Hustler* magazines and underground fight clubs.

For I am a Man.
I praise Spartan culture for being so masculine.
But I beat my son for wearing some eyeliner, puny faggot.

You're starting to understand.

Because as a man who needs logic or reason?

We speak with our fist.

As a Man, who needs comfort when we find ourselves in the reflection of the bottom of our liquor bottle?
Because as a Man, why would we ask for help when we can do it ourselves?
For I am a Man.

Moments That Make Me Want to Write Poetry

Sometimes it's a cliche feeling when I see a beautiful sunset
A dad walking with his son
The way the trees look as wind blows through

Sometimes it's a terrifying emotion that comes with the anxiety of cold and hot air playing the most lethal game of tag
Or a man acting out of animalistic nature

But then, there are those rare moments
Those once in a lifetime moments that make you feel like you've experienced a moment in history that will be sung about
Those moments are what make me passionate about writing

And of course I'm talking about the moments with you
The times in the shower when the perfect song is playing and I can't keep from making eye contact
When we are slow dancing to a trashy song when blue and green lights cast an aura around you looking like a scene ripped from a Euphoria episode
Or even when you watch movies with me

You, love, make me want to write poetry.

Masculinity

At my place of occupation I remained upright like a monument of a tragic battleground
The ghost around speaking with loose tongues and words soaked in napalm

I hear a saying float across the room like tear gas at a peaceful protest,
"If it bleeds for seven days and is still alive you shouldn't trust it."

This took me by shock,
not the "Dang that was profound, I've never thought of it that way"
More like, "You ignorant, good for nothing, sexist, misogynistic…"
you get the idea

The phrase came from a "man," and I say that with little respect, a "man" standing like a swastika does beside the bible
He was standing the way a bullet casing stands in front of a mother who just lost her child to a school shooting
He stood there the way Stalin did when the words, "Cannot even shoot straight" escaped his vile mouth and attacked his child's mind
Reflecting on the incident, I began to realize, what he said does not matter.
At the end of the day, none of his actions matter.
But this event will play in my mind over and over. It will remind me work needs to be done.

Paranoia I

When every man seeks the woman you're with
you look over your shoulder at every turn
You pay attention to every pair of eyes in the room
You listen to conversations
You watch their body language

You know what they want
You know their goal
You know what they will do to get to it

You know all of this, because you did it yourself.

FILE:10.14.21.

We shared a common value of ink displayed on skin to reflect our inner thoughts subtly
After work you met me at the church beside my house
We told each other things that no one knew about us and this was the first time we met outside of work
Now, not to be dramatic, but it was something beautiful
You speak of home and fallen passions along with a broken heart
You couldn't tell, but I knew your darkest secret just by the way you communicated your interest
We sat on the hood of your '05 Mustang and talked for about two hours
I never expected us to be where we are today
I never expected to fall so deep
But with every word that rolled off my tongue it felt like the phrase, "I Do" was itching to escape
I don't believe in love
I don't believe in "the one."
But what I do know is that night we met, I knew you were going to be my girlfriend, and I knew you would be a permanent role in my life.

Watching Movies

In the moments where we find ourselves wrapped in each other's voice

The moments when Mac Miller's vocals hangs over us like my curfew

The moments when I feel so close to you that your heartbeat causes shockwaves through my rib cage

Those moments is where I find something as powerful as love

We were watching Good Will Hunting

You told me you loved it

The joy that brought me

A movie I feel so connected to

A movie I find so relatable

And you loved it

I hope that means you don't lie when you tell me you love me.

My Definition of Love

You told me that you think love is our conversations late night at work, but I think it's the opposite.
I think our love is the subtle pauses between each word and phrase that has such an emphasis that we hold on to each precarious syllable like our life depends on it
I think our love is dilated pupils with a smirk on our face
I think our love falls deep like ink in skin and lyrics to the heart
I think our love is found between paragraphs that we send as the other sleeps
I think our love can be seen most at night when we take turns holding each other because we know it helps the other sleep

Love, I find you in every song
I see you when I read every poem
I feel for you when I can tell you're in pain

You are my person
I will always love you for that
You are worth adapting for
You are worth effort
You are worth risk
You are worth loving something more than myself

8.3.1.

I am sorry,
I know at the time of reading this you will not understand
Moving, well more like floating
Blissfully through life one argument at a time

I apologize for not being perfect
I apologize for not understanding
and I apologize for hurting you

The fear of losing you in my life consumes my subconscious like a grizzly finding wounded prey, viciously...
You have impacted me in so many ways and I cannot comprehend what my life would be like without you

That is why I am terrified
but, life is about risk
You are a risk
but a risk that is worth it

I know I do a lot of things that upset you
Texting her
Yelling
Substance use
Sleeping when I'm supposed to come over

I understand
I really do
even when I'm frustrated, I promise I get it

You are worth the effort
You are worth the time
and You above all things
are
worth
the
Love

You are my person.

I hope when she looks at Him

she thinks of Me

because I am just That pretty.

Honesty Vol.2

I think it's time that I was completely transparent for you
Now I claimed to be honest and vulnerable, which was true, far more than I have been with anyone else
But I am at heart a paranoid child locking away his emotions to protect himself and those around him
Sadly this "safe" also has a self-destruct button and you, my love, were caught in the fallout
You poor soul,

See, what I don't believe you could ever grasp is how often I was protecting you from yourself.
We share a common feature in being self-destructive but in different ways
You are physically and mentally destructive. You sacrifice so much of yourself to gain so little.
Sex is thrown away for drugs
Time is spent to combat loneliness
Nudes are sent to grasp validation

You lack so much love,
For yourself
I wanted nothing more to show you that you were worth loving...
But not for us
For you
To protect you
Because as long as I could make you think you had worth, you stayed from him
The longer I kept you the longer you had him blocked

But in the end what does it matter if the story's conclusion is you on your knees for him

I'm so sorry I couldn't convince you...

Survivor's Guilt

The pain I'm feeling is beyond that of a simple prescription from a psychiatrist
I am stuck in purgatory relieving the same day as punishment for my sins
Like a dog chasing his tail

I thought I'd be a better man
I thought I had changed, grown, but in the end I am only my father's son

You have succumbed to your pain and given in to that of mortal pleasure
I have to stand and watch the train wreck happen

You are killing yourself because of my actions and for that I am sorry.

My House is Burning

Flames crawl on the walls around me.
Photographs of a family that never was—turned to ash.
Smoke invades my lungs, I choke on my sins.

I hear the screams of those I love in the other room
Vocal cords stretching in hopes of some form of salvation even if that very salvation is death.
Fibers violate fingernails as they scrape in agony.

The circle of fire that surrounds me is reminiscent of Dante's comedy.
I am encompassed by pain and suffering.
I can hear the misery.
I feel remorse.
But why am I holding the match?

Sign of the Times

She

Bright lights shine across a wave of people
Black crows and golden doves fly above
Religious chants for an abundant harvest

I float in the middle, stuck in a cosmogyral.
Lightning flowing through my veins
Heart pumping with the rhythm of the crowd.

When I look at you, everything around me crumbles to dust and I get high off the powder.
The crows above feast on my narcissism and rage
While the doves sing songs of pulp.

When I hear your laugh—time stops.
I see old paintings from epic artists of the past.
I can hear the scraping of graphite on canvas.
I can smell the paint as it dries on the chapel.
I can feel the water as it cleanses the mistakes made.

Oh love, when I think of you, I print missing posters just to know you're looking for me!
I fumble over the words I'm saying in hopes of you catching me when I fall.
I gathered my pride, my envy, my lust, and my greed and threw a party just so I could invite you.
I make a playlist with songs that make me think of you hoping you'll spring out of my screen and provide me with the warmth I feel when I hear your voice.

I swear when the Greeks found Medusa and thought she was the perfect woman, they were a few centuries too early because I'm looking at you now and I am petrified.
Now I know this may seem theatrical, but I swear when we talk, I can feel the next sixty years of my life with you.

So why is it that when your friends ask about me you say, "Oh, he's just a friend"?

I found God in the backseat of my friend's car wearing a black and white flannel and some killer mascara

In the corner of my room, you will find a scared fish writing his fourth suicide note that week
In my dresser, you may find my wings clipped for a romantic gesture.
On my counter, you will find a picture frame
Golden from side to side, its reflection twists and bends
Hung like a smile it shows its razor teeth
Hands shaky afraid to touch
But almost salivating at the idea of finding myself.

I couldn't resist
Draped in Motley, I introduce myself.
Long legs
Brown hair
Button nose
Cute face
Listening to "The Neighborhood" in her wired headphones while the world collapses behind her.
Her lips curl at the edge mimicking the Milky Way—soft, but powerful.
Her eyes can pierce you like an arrow but you hope she doesn't miss.
Her voice cradles your body like a blanket of spiderwebs—
entrapping you,
but so warm you don't want to leave.

Her hands run through my hair causing a chain reaction leading to a thunderstorm in my chest.

My hand around her throat with a touch so gentle like I was afraid she would break.

Holding this marvel so close to me as if I was scared to share her perfection with the world.

She smiled and tattooed, "Call out my name" on the back of my hand so I can't touch another girl without thinking of her.

Dream

I found your presence comforting,
A prize worth protecting
Your lips met mine like an inspired author with a pen
My hands caressing the curves of your body like I could sift gold
from them
The affection I felt was new,
Foreign
Dare I say, extraterrestrial?
Dare I call it,
Love.

You look so pretty under the black light hanging above me

Blue reflection off of translucent strands of hair.
Some Indie movie you've never heard of plays in the background.
Curled lips smile at me as I lift your chin.
Eyes lock in an eternal exchange.
Champagne soaks your voice and I'm drunk off your laugh.

My bed feels better with you in it.
Movies are more enjoyable when I watch them with you.
Lyrics are deeper when I share them with you.

Personally, I've never been big on physical touch,
but my hand has never felt as lonely as it does without yours.

You are an addiction that makes me scratch "sober"
out of every dictionary I can find.

Overprotective

His eyes met mine.
I could see his intentions hidden in the details of his iris.
Smoke left his body with his humanity following suit.
An animalistic need clashing with morality.

We sit in our booth.
The man stayed outside, eyes occasionally meeting at the intersection between the scales of candor

My fear and pride join us at our booth.
She sits in front of me alone.
My one goal is her safety, but how can I manage to fight off an animal if I can't fight my own fear of the thought?

He lurks around the counter, probably counting down the time for his attack.
Frightened by his composure, I made her aware of my concern.

Now fear ravages our bodies like a new disease that can't be cured.

That overbearing feeling of powerlessness that consumes your every thought—pumping adrenaline through your body

I've never felt so close with death.

Powerless

We censor our education.
We silence our children.
And we disembowel our cities.

I stand in a white forest filled with creatures of the night
We move cognitively as a hive.

The pervert has his crosshair on my lungs with lust on his trigger finger.
He licks his lips at the thought of it.

A bullet forced through my body stealing something from me that was never his to begin with.
My killer won't remember my name, but he will never forget my taste.

What am I to do when he has his hand on my head with a knife to my throat?

Hate Me

Posting about me doesn't fill the absence of feelings for one another
Shit talking about me doesn't stop my life from continuing
Fucking people close to me will not shatter my reality

All you've done is validate my reasons for leaving.

Candor

I need to make it explicit that your intent was clear
You want me heartbroken and crying
You thought it would devastate me

Late nights together putting on fake faces as if it were a masquerade
Childish suggestions and excuses
Silver Tongue succubus spitting Hennessy words for me to drink from your lips
You must think me a fool to fall for your tricks
But, love, I know everything,
I heard the ringtones
I smelled the cologne
I saw the marks
I could feel the emotion
It's okay.

Sex

Sex, it's a straightforward process.
Very basic, can be complicated with the wrong person
A transaction of sorts
By which I mean
You are trading your body for their intimacy
A currency like no other for the momentary feeling that you are loved

Now, a person can give you their body. They can do everything you want. Any fantasy you have, they can do it all.

But they can do every single thing they did with you to someone else
Now as cynical as that sounds it is still truth

But that's why sex CAN have intimacy and it CAN be loving

But what's really good
What REALLY makes my skin crawl is the deep conversations after
That's the good stuff
The truly valuable currency
Like I said they can do all of those great and wonderfully amazing things with you and someone else
But the things they tell you can never be delivered the same way

When you ask them about their hopes and dreams, that sparkle in their eye will never shine the same as it did when they told you

When you ask them their greatest fear, their heart will never beat at the same pace
When they tell you their past, their breaths will never move in that rhythm

That to me is intimacy.

Self-Destructive Nature

I toss myself into sunken pits known as "DMs"
Unapologetically myself delivering this profound image of someone who couldn't care less
Attracting those that feel the same
Late night talks
Meaningless Sex
Boyfriends who haven't the slightest idea of how you've been touching me
At the end of the day, I'm going to continue this game of cat and mouse
In between liquor bottles and used trojans you somehow find a way to let the three-word phrase crawl from your lips
I almost can't resist, and it appears that's a mutual feeling.

Self-Loathing.

Bragging to my brother that I'm "5 for 5" at work
Doesn't it really matter if you got their snap
Does it really matter if they're DTF
At the end of the day you're going to be laying in your bed
Alone
and
They will be crawling back in bed with their boyfriend

Was it just a pitty fuck?

Behind the mask of every poet is a child trying to piece their puzzle together.

Lavender,

Do the stars look the same from your perspective?
I was at a party for lost souls and crushed dreams
Depressed kids meeting in a congregation of fire in hopes of
purging their desperation
I missed you there,
This place didn't deserve your presence
You were far too good for the setting, but
I missed you nonetheless
Stupid children, we were drinking away the void that fills our
hearts, but even liquid love could not cure the curse of being "God's
Lonely Man"
Thank you for the time we've spent. I hope to write many more
with you in mind.

The Law of Blonde

Multiversal Rejection

We remain precarious over a pit of "I miss you"s and "I hate you"s
The toxic waste that spills from my mouth into our reality infects those around me
Like a game of Russian roulette we point and shoot not thinking of the consequences

I'm still looking for the key to escape the cage I've put myself in
Maybe it's your pheromones, maybe your eyes, maybe your tone
But every time you cross my sight, I throw the key back into the abyss from whence it came

Somewhere
there is a reality
where we remain
in the trunk of charcoal gray jeep
lying beside our Aussie
with *our* song playing over the sound system
looking out on to the sunrise over a lake in Maine

Socially Acceptable Self-Harm

Cuts to a wrist
Burns to flesh
Starving yourself to the point of your body eating itself to survive,

I must have 2,700 calories
168 grams of protein
and 102 ounces of water in a day

Monday, can't miss arms
If I can't push past 25s on dumbbells then I'm going to hurt myself with the thoughts of her, but as long as I'm getting my gains right

To make sure I can reach my max on bench force music from your days of suicidal thoughts like a drill into your eardrums to make the pain fuel your body

Trial by fire to force myself to fit my image of a man
Flimsy arms
Chicken Legs
Noodle boy,

Pathetic.

Needle to skin is usually looked down upon, but when filled with ink you're somehow a badass for taking the pain?

Forcing myself to sit for hours in a chair with a complete stranger because I'm not comfortable enough with sharing my personal thoughts so I force them to my skin as a way of somehow just maybe someone will see my cry for help

But sick ink, right? Talk about that line work,

Now comparing body counts like they're a currency more valuable than gold

Holding up the hottest one under your belt like it was a trophy to be worshipped

Giving yourself to a complete stranger in hopes of being validated by your friends because you are not comfortable in your own skin
You do not think you're deserving of real love, so you force yourself to become a sex toy for others to enjoy, because if they love the sex they love you, right?

"Did you see her ass, man? You couldn't hit that if you tried."

Fuck, You.

Sometimes I think I hate you,
Not for any petty reason
Not because I didn't get my way
Not because you chose him

It's because you showed me reality
You showed me the truth

I had this airbrushed fantasy of us living happily ever after in some cute cabin in Maine with an Aussie
When you were planning your wedding out with him

We were buying groceries in my mind
While you were saying your vows

We were watching horror movies on the couch
While you were raising his child

I don't hate you for being happy
I hate you because you didn't need me for that

You

I can't seem to find the right pattern or formula of mixing vowels and consonants to describe exactly how I feel about you

Let me put it this way,
You know the overwhelming emotion you get when looking at classic paintings? That's where I find you

Or maybe even that dreadful chill down your spine when you think about commitment, that's you

Hold up, That warm feeling over alcohol as it travels through your body, potent, euphoric, that's you

You are my cyanide capsule, you may decide the context of that

You bring out the best of my worst self,

You are the 808s on Kanye's Old tracks

You are my exception in the Law of Blonde

You are the only person I've seen make a button-down look that good

You are Baby Gap's number one shopper

You are addictive

You are the inspiration for "Divine Feminine"
You are everything I want, but exactly what I can't have...

You.ii.

You are what makes the roof of my mouth itch for a barrel

I used to be such a nice guy
I fell out of love with photography,
Drawing,
Life
Now it's just,
You

The lust for our life together consumes me
Hellfire spits from my mouth and burns the bridges around me

Maybe I'll be worthy of the title "damsel in distress"
You could be my Knight in Shiny lingerie

Darling, what I see in your eyes is a dilated void that feeds on my dependence

Because the fatal cuts on my wrist are worth the blood of the lamb so here I stand awaiting my judgment

enjoy it
You sick fuck.

I don't know where I stand with you,
all I know is that when I fall,
I hope you catch me.

Dare I call it Poetry?

Slow dancing to the rhythm of our heartbeats but droning off-key listening to our brain waves

falling over the lies spit from my forked tongue

Tripping over the fairy tales you told to me,

We used to be everything

met at a young age,
Knew when you walked in the door

Building this fantasy of something more than what we were,
We are only our parents' children,

Emotions so strong they could split an atom
So powerful they could level a city
So colossal they could create life

Dare I call it a Weapon?

Dare I call it Destructive?
Dare I call it Innovation?

No, no something's this powerful can only be fueled by emotion an emotion so corrosive it dissolves the flesh leaving only the skeleton you tried to hide in your closet
An emotion so vile it corrupts minds and kills dreams

Dare I call it hate?

But to say that you have a feeling as raw and foul as hate
You must first
Have an emotion equally powerful to cause this reaction
Dare I call it chemistry?

This is to say you cannot have hate alone, Hate is constructed
Hate must fester
Hate must build
Hate must swell
Hate comes from something so beautiful
Something pure
Something timeless

Dare I call it Love?